A New True Book

WHALES AND OTHER SEA MAMMALS

By Elsa Posell

This "true book" was prepared
under the direction of
Illa Podendorf,
formerly with the Laboratory School,
University of Chicago

CHILDRENS PRESS ®

CHICAGO

Leaping bottlenose dolphins

PHOTO CREDITS

© Marine Mammal Fund—cover, 9, 13, 40, 43;
© Robert Pitman, 2; © 1980 Rich Sears, 6, 7, 22,
24, © 1979 Blue Whale Expedition, 18; © Stan
Minasian, 25, 35 (left)

Mark Rosenthal—11

© James M. Cribb—34, 35 (left), 36 (left)

Louise T. Lunak—14, 45

Lynn M. Stone—35 (right)

Whaling Museum Society, Inc.—16, 38, 39

Reinhard Brucker—33 (left)

Len Meents—4, 21, 23, 27

Miami Seaquarium—28 (2 photos), 30, 31,
33 (right), 36 (right)

COVER—Blue Whale and baby

Library of Congress Cataloging in Publication Data

Posell, Elsa Z.
  Whales and other sea mammals.

  (A New true book)
  Previously published as: The true book of whales and
other sea mammals. 1963.
  Includes index.
  Summary: Briefly covers the characteristics, types,
young, and relatives of whales and discusses the
hunting and protection of these giants of the sea.
    1. Whales—Juvenile literature. [1. Whales]
I. Title.
QL737.C4P67 1982   599.5   82-4451
ISBN 0-516-01663-6   AACR2

TABLE OF CONTENTS

Diplodocus

Blue Whale

Horse

GIANTS OF THE SEA

Some whales are bigger than any dinosaurs that people know about.

Some people believe that millions of years ago whales had legs and lived on land.

They would have been smaller then. They may have been the size of a large dinosaur or even an elephant.

Humpback whale

Nobody knows when or why whales became sea animals instead of land animals.

Whales can be very large since they live in the sea. Water helps hold up the weight of their huge bodies.

Whales do not have many enemies because they are so big.

Some whales may live twenty years or longer. The fin whale may live eighty years.

Back of fin whale as it dives

Whales can dive deep into the sea. The sperm whale can dive as deep as two miles.

Whales live, feed, and often play in groups in many different oceans.

Whales travel far. They are always moving about looking for food.

They have large, flat, tail-like flukes. Their flukes help them move through the water.

Tail, or flukes, of a gray whale

They do not fight among themselves. A whale seldom attacks a boat unless the whale has been wounded.

WHALES ARE MAMMALS

Whales are not fish.

Fish breathe through gills. They are cold-blooded animals. They have scales and are hatched from eggs.

Whales are mammals. All mammals are warm-blooded. They have hair or fur and lungs. Their young are born and drink milk from their mother's body.

A whale has smooth skin and a few bristles of hair around its mouth.

For ears, a whale has only a small hole on each side of its head.

The eyes of a whale are small, too. There is one on each side of the head.

Beluga whale

HOW WHALES BREATHE

Most whales come up for air about every seven or eight minutes. Some whales may stay down for as long as an hour.

Whales breathe through blowholes in the top of their heads. Blowholes are tightly shut when whales are underwater. They open only when whales come up to breathe.

Blue whale blowing

Whales blow warm air
out through the blowholes.
The warm air looks like
fog when it hits the cold
air.

Spouts of two whales at sea

A whale does not breathe through its mouth. There is no opening between the throat and the lungs of a whale. The mouth is for eating.

A whale can eat under-water without getting water into its lungs.

HOW WHALES KEEP WARM

Since whales are mammals and are warm-blooded, they must have a way to keep warm.

Some animals have fur.

People wear clothes to keep warm.

Whales have blubber.

Blubber is a thick layer of fat under the skin.

Whales that live in icy waters have more blubber than those that live in warmer waters. Blubber also helps keep a whale from starving if food is scarce.

BABY WHALES

A baby whale is called a calf.

The calf can swim when it is born. But for more than half a year it stays close to its mother and drinks her warm milk.

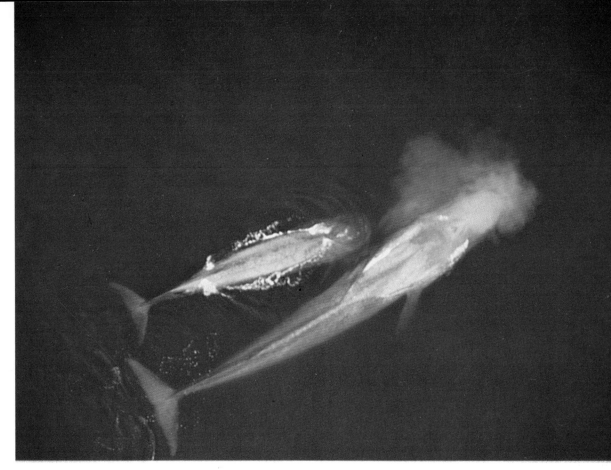

Blue whale and baby

A new-born sulphur-
bottom or blue whale calf
may be larger than a full-
grown elephant.

A year-old calf is twice
as big as it was when it
was born.

A mother whale takes
care of her calf. If the calf
is wounded, the mother
may be captured because
she will not leave her
baby.

KINDS OF WHALES

There are two main groups of whales. One group has teeth and the other does not.

Baleen whales have no teeth. Sheets of hornlike baleen hang from the roofs of their mouths.

A baleen whale swims along with its mouth open. It catches shrimps or other small sea animals. The baleen closes like a gate. The whale pushes the sea-water out through the baleen and swallows the food.

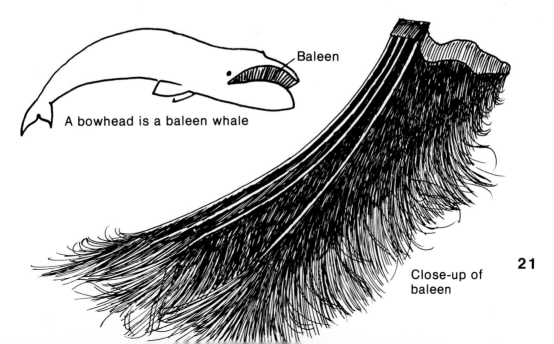

Baleen

A bowhead is a baleen whale

Close-up of baleen

Baleen whales often find food close to the surface of the water.

The largest whales are baleen whales. Even though they are large animals, their throat openings are small.

A baleen whale has two blowholes in the top of its head.

The blowholes of a humpback whale

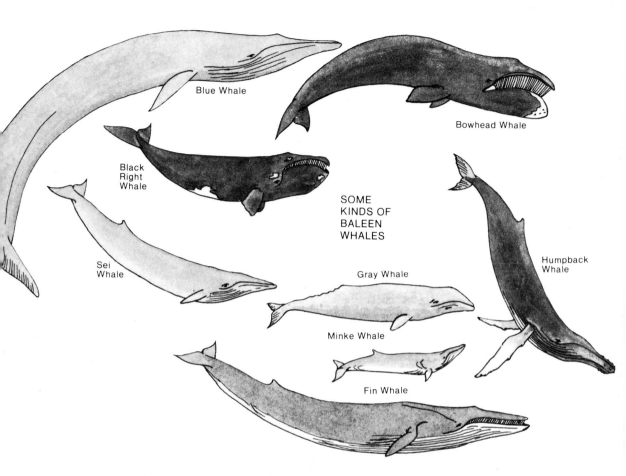

Blue Whale

Bowhead Whale

Black Right Whale

SOME KINDS OF BALEEN WHALES

Humpback Whale

Sei Whale

Gray Whale

Minke Whale

Fin Whale

In the baleen group are the bowheads, right whales, gray whales, humpback whales, the blue whales, and others.

The humpback whale is thirty-five to fifty feet long. It looks clumsy, but it is a very fast swimmer. Like many of the baleen whales, it has ridges on the underside of its body.

A humpback whale about to slap its tail on the water

Two, eighty-five-foot blue whales

The blue whale is also called the sulphur-bottom because of the thousands of tiny, yellow sea creatures that grow on its underside.

The blue whale is the largest of all whales. It may be seventy-five to a hundred feet long.

The right whale is forty to sixty feet long. It got its name in the early days of whaling. It was just "right" to catch. It was not fast. It was easy to get it to the boat because it did not sink after it was killed.

The largest toothed whale is smaller than the largest baleen whale.

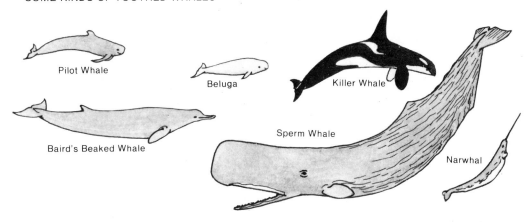

SOME KINDS OF TOOTHED WHALES

Pilot Whale

Beluga

Killer Whale

Baird's Beaked Whale

Sperm Whale

Narwhal

Some of the toothed whales have only two or four teeth. Some have fifty or more. The sharp teeth help them to catch their food.

They often dive deep to get cuttlefish and giant squid.

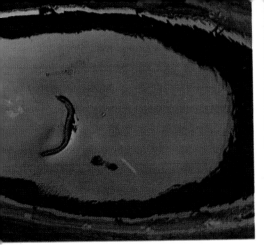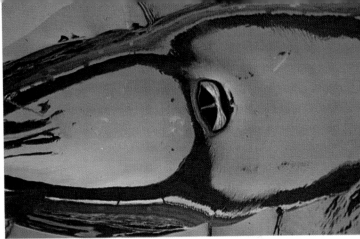

Close-up of the blowholes of a killer whale—closed (left) and open (right)

A toothed whale has only one blowhole in the top of its head.

The sperm whale, largest of the toothed whales, is forty to sixty feet long.

The big, square head of a sperm whale takes up about one third of its length.

Twenty to thirty sharp teeth in the lower jaw fit into pits in the upper jaw.

A sperm whale is not as large as some of the baleen whales. But its throat is bigger than the throats of other kinds of whales.

A sperm whale will dive deep to get a giant squid.

A killer whale is only twenty to thirty feet long. It is black except for the white on its neck and belly.

Killer
whale

This whale has large, curved teeth in both upper and lower jaws. It will eat anything that crosses its path: birds, fish, walruses, porpoises.

Killer whales are fast swimmers. They hunt in packs and they will attack even the biggest whales.

WHALE RELATIVES

A dolphin is seven to thirty feet long. It is in the toothed whale family and has as many as a hundred teeth in each jaw.

Some dolphins are dark brown or black on top and lighter underneath. Freshwater dolphins are gray and white all over.

A porpoise is related to the dolphin. It is smaller and its snout is more blunt.

Playful and smart, porpoises (left) and dolphins (above) are often called "sea clowns."

Porpoises are often seen near shore. They swim in large schools and eat many mackerel and herring.

Harbor seals, mother and pup

Seals are related to whales.

Some are hunted for their fur and for oil.

Sea lions belong to the eared-seal family. Their fur is not so good.

Seals and sea lions spend part of the time out of water.

Seals (left) and walrus (above)
are related to whales.

The walrus is a sea
mammal that lives in
northern waters.

These manatees are sometimes called sea cows.

Manatees and dugongs are plant-eating mammals of the sea.

The manatee lives in warm Atlantic waters. The dugong is found near the East Indies and Australia.

WHALE HUNTING LONG AGO

For hundreds of years, men risked their lives to hunt for whales.

Tall-masted sailing ships sometimes stayed at sea for two or three years on a whale hunt.

Three-masted whaling ship

"There she blows!" was
the cry of the lookout on
the mast who sighted a
whale.

Small boats were lowered. While some men rowed, one stood ready to throw his harpoon.

This was dangerous. Sometimes the harpooned whale raced through the water, pulling the boats after it.

This fin whale has just been harpooned and is close to death. The whaling boat moves in to haul the animal aboard.

WHALE HUNTING TODAY

Now whale hunting is not so dangerous. Big ships called "factories" go to sea with smaller, whale-catcher boats.

Helicopters spot the whales. The news is sent by radio. The whale-catcher boats go after the whale. A gun fires a large harpoon.

The whale is then taken to the factory ship.

At the factory ship, the whale is cut up. Its meat is wrapped and cooled immediately.

Whale bones are made into fertilizer.

Today only the sperm whale is killed for its oil.

A seventy-ton sperm whale yields about fifteen barrels of oil from its huge head.

A waxy solid taken from the head of a sperm whale is used to make fine candles.

Whale oil is used in many ways. Soap and cosmetics are made from it. A spread for bread can be made from the oil, too.

Whale meat is eaten in Japan, Norway, and Greenland.
Japan leads the world in whale hunting today.

An adult gray whale raises its head out of the water.

WHALES ARE PROTECTED

There was a danger of killing too many whales with the new ways of whale hunting.

Several nations met and made some whaling rules.

Whaling boats may catch only a certain number of whales each year.

Whales that are not full grown are not to be killed.

A gray whale allows itself to be petted.

Mother whales with calves are not to be killed.

There is to be no whale hunting in some parts of the oceans.

Whaling boats are to be watched to make sure the laws are obeyed.

WORDS YOU SHOULD KNOW

Australia(awss • TRAYL • ya) —one of the seven continents.
baleen(bay • LEEN) —horn-like material found in the mouth of some whales instead of teeth.
blubber(BLUB • er) —the thick layer of fat under the skin of whales and other sea animals.
blunt(BLUHNT) —not sharp or pointed.
bristle(BRISS • il) —short, stiff hair.
cosmetic(koz • MEH • tic) —something like a lotion or powder used on the body.
cuttlefish(CUT • il • fish) —water animal related to the octopus.
dolphin(DOLL • fin) —a sea animal related to whales.
dugong(DOO • gong) —a sea mammal.
East Indies(EEST IN • deez) —a group of islands in the Pacific Ocean.
enemy(EN • eh • me) —not a friend.
fertilizer(FER • tih • lye • zer) —something added to soil to help plants grow.
fluke(FLOOK) —part of the tail of a whale.
harpoon(har • POON) —a spear with a rope attached to it used in hunting whales.
herring(HAIR • ing) —a kind of fish used by man as food.
huge(HYOOJ) —very large.
mackerel(MACK • ril) —an ocean fish that man uses as food.
manatee(MAN • ah • tee) —a sea mammal.
mast —a tall pole that holds the sails on a sailboat.

obey(oh • BAY) — to listen to; follow orders.

pit — a small hole.

porpoise(POR • puss) — a sea animal related to whales.

ridge(RIJ) — narrow, raised strip.

scarce(SCARE • ss) — hard to get or find.

school — a large group of fish or other water animals swimming together.

seldom(SELL • dum) — not often; rarely.

snout — long nose.

squid(SKWID) — a sea animal related to the octopus.

walrus(WALL • russ) — a large sea mammal related to seals.

warm-blooded — having blood that doesn't change temperature.

INDEX

About the Author

Elsa Posell received her M.S. in Library Science from Western Reserve University. She has been a librarian in the Cleveland Heights Public Schools, and is currently devoting over half her time to work with children in the Cleveland area and other Ohio counties in language arts, story telling, and creative writing. As a story teller and lecturer Mrs. Posell has worked in schools in Korea, Japan, Hong Kong, and China. One of her books, This is an Orchestra, *is published in Japanese. Mrs. Posell is also the author of* American Composers, Russian Music and Musicians, Russian Authors, *and* Beginning Book of Knowledge of Seashells.